Arranged by Dan Coates

M000107431

New POP Music

For the Elementary Player

1999 Edition

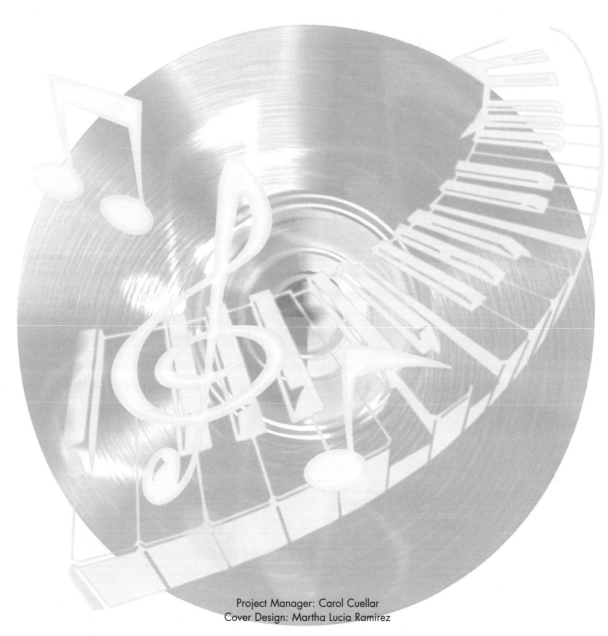

Project Manager: Carol Cuellar
Cover Design: Martha Lucia Ramirez

Dan Coates

One of today's foremost personalities in the field of printed music, Dan Coates has been providing teachers and professional musicians with quality piano material since 1975. Equally adept in arranging for beginners or accomplished musicians, his Big Note, Easy Piano and Professional Touch arrangements have made a significant contribution to the industry.

Born in Syracuse, New York, Dan began to play piano at the age of four. By the time he was 15, he'd won a New York State competition for music composers. After high school graduation, he toured the United States, Canada and Europe as an arranger and pianist with the world-famous group Up With People.

Dan settled in Miami, Florida, where he studied piano with Ivan Davis at the University of Miami while playing professionally throughout southern Florida. To date, his performance credits include appearances on "Murphy Brown" and "My Sister Sam" and at the Opening Ceremonies of the 1984 Summer Olympics in Los Angeles. Dan has also accompanied such artists as Dusty Springfield and Charlotte Rae.

In 1982, Dan began his association with Warner Bros. Publications—an association that has produced more than four hundred Dan Coates books and sheets. Throughout the year, he conducts piano workshops nationwide, during which he demonstrates his popular arrangements.

Contents

ALL MY LIFE

Words and Music by
RORY BENNETT and
JO JO HAILEY
Arranged by DAN COATES

6

7

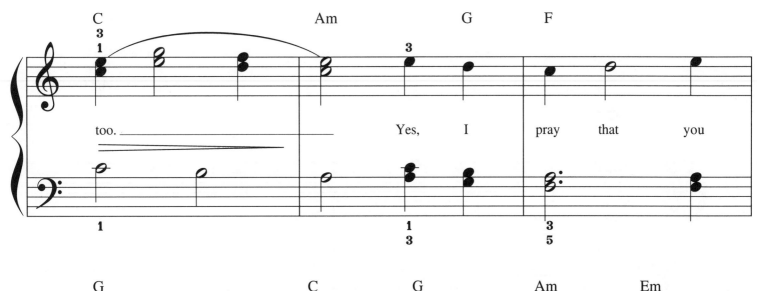

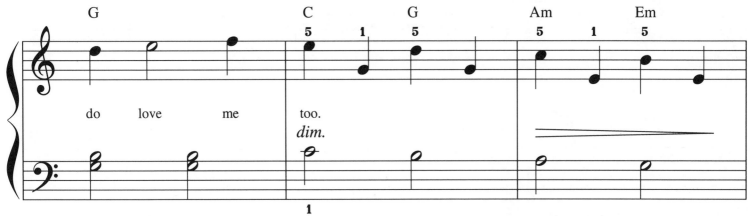

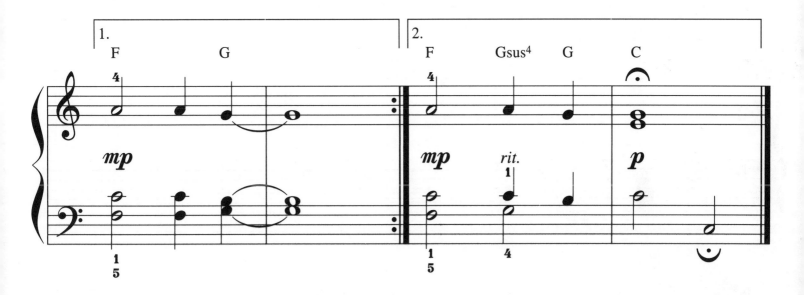

Verse 2:
I promise to never fall in love with a stranger.
You're all I'm thinking of,
I praise the Lord above
For sending me your love.
I cherish every hug.
I really love you so much.
(To Chorus:)

All My Life - 4 - 4

ANGEL EYES

Composed by
JIM BRICKMAN
Arranged by DAN COATES

Brightly

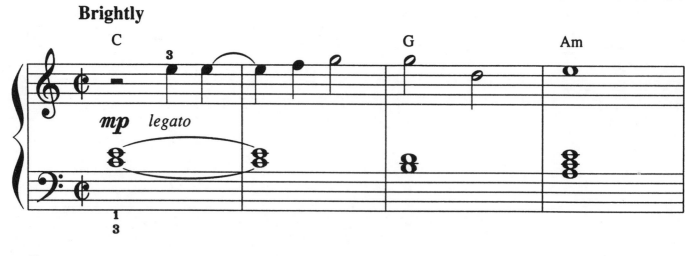

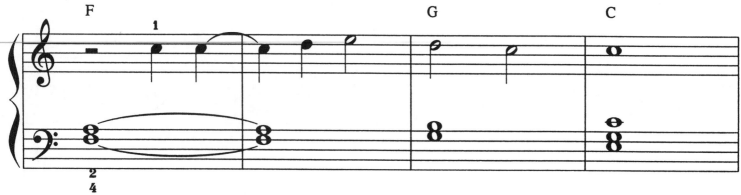

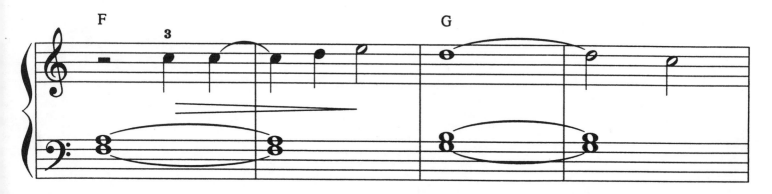

Angel Eyes - 4 - 1

10

Angel Eyes - 4 - 3

ANGEL OF MINE

Words and Music by
RHETT LAWRENCE and TRAVON POTTS
Arranged by DAN COATES

Moderately, with feeling

14

Angel of Mine - 4 - 3

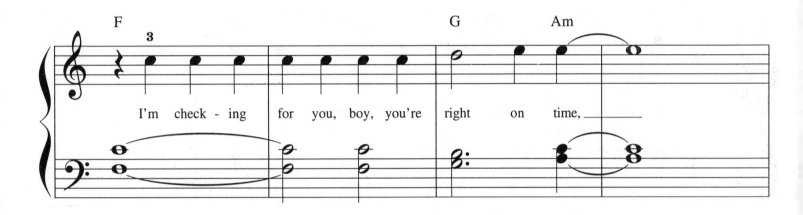

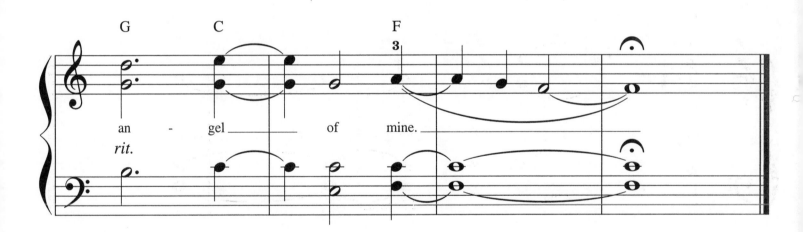

Verse 2:
I look at you looking at me.
Now I know why they say the best things are free.
I'm gonna love you, boy, you are so fine,
Angel of mine.

Verse 3:
Nothing means more to me than what we share.
No one in this whole world can ever compare.
Last night, the way you moved is still on my mind,
Angel of mine.

From the Twentieth Century Fox Motion Picture
"ANASTASIA"

AT THE BEGINNING

Lyrics by
LYNN AHERNS

Music by
STEPHEN FLAHERTY
Arranged by DAN COATES

Moderate rock ballad

1. We were stran - gers start - ing out on a jour -
2. No one told me I was go - ing to find

ney,
you.
nev - er dream - ing what we'd have to go through.
Un - ex - pect - ed, what you did to my heart.

Now here we are and I'm sud - den - ly stand -
When I lost hope, you were there to re - mind

I'll be there when the world stops turn - ing, I'll be there when the storm is through.

To Coda ⊕

In the end, I want to be stand - ing at the be - gin - ning with

1.

you.

2.

you.

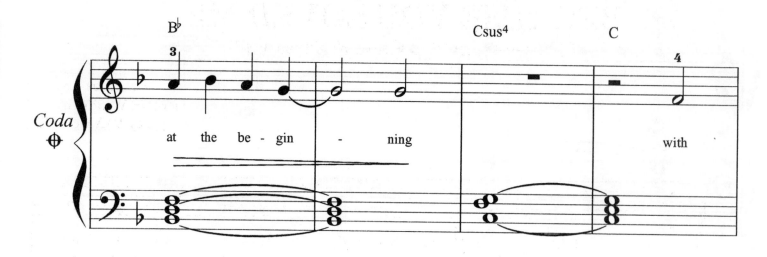

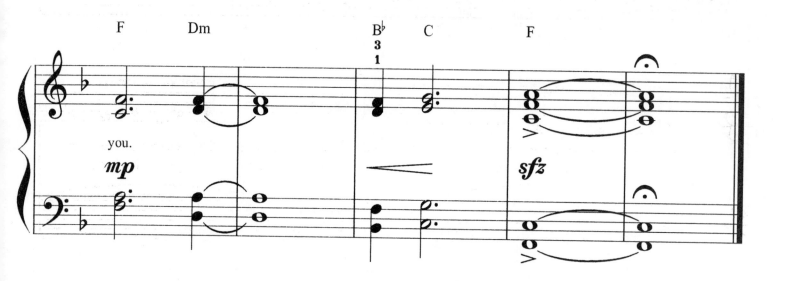

Verse 3:
We were strangers
On a crazy adventure,
Never dreaming
How our dream would come true.
Now here we stand
Unafraid of the future,
At the beginning with you.
(To Chorus:)

BECAUSE YOU LOVED ME
(Theme from "Up Close & Personal")

Words and Music by
DIANE WARREN
Arranged by DAN COATES

23

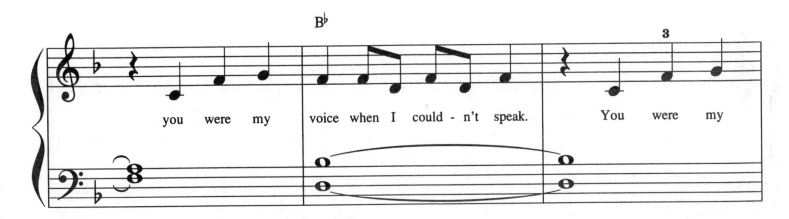

you were my voice when I could-n't speak. You were my

eyes when I could-n't see, you saw the best there was ___ in me.

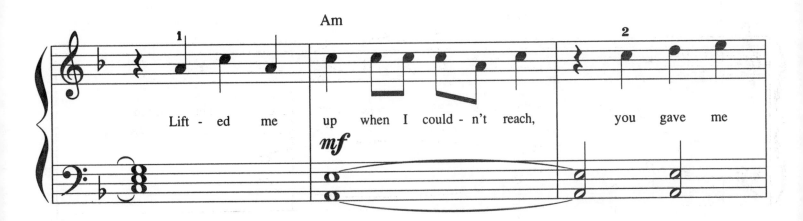

Lift-ed me up when I could-n't reach, you gave me

faith 'cause you ___ be - lieved. I'm ev-'ry-thing ___ I am

Because You Loved Me - 5 - 3

24

BECAUSE OF YOU

Words and Music by
ANDERS BAGGE, ARNTHOR BIRGISSON,
CHRISTIAN KARLSSON and PATRICK TUCKER
Arranged by DAN COATES

28

Because of You - 4 - 3

Verse 2:
Honestly, could it be you and me
Like it was before, need less or more?
'Cause when I close my eyes at night,
I realize that no one else
Could ever take your place.

I still can feel, and it's so real,
When you're touching me,
Kisses endlessly.
It's just a place in the sun
Where our love's begun.
I miss you, yes I miss you.
(To Chorus:)

BUTTERFLY KISSES

Words and Music by
BOB CARLISLE and **RANDY THOMAS**
Arranged by DAN COATES

Slowly and tenderly

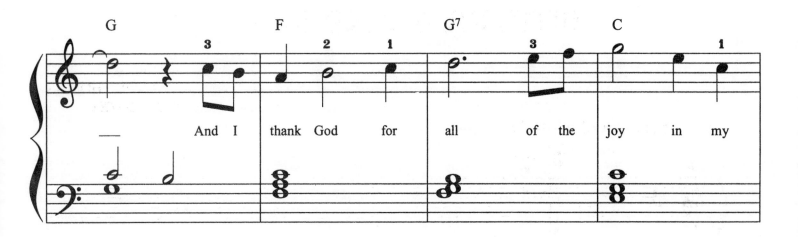

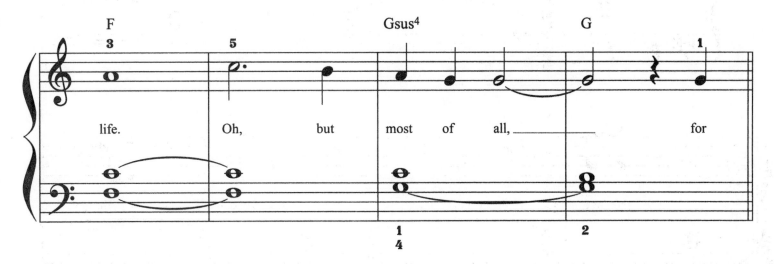

Chorus:

32

D.S. %. al Coda

Coda

Verse 2:
Sweet sixteen today,
She's lookin' like her mama a little more every day.
One part woman, the other part girl;
To perfume and make-up from ribbons and curls.
Trying her wings out in a great big world.
But I remember:

Chorus 2:
Butterfly kisses after bedtime prayer,
Stickin' little white flowers all up in her hair.
"You know how much I love you, daddy,
But if you don't mind,
I'm only gonna kiss you on the cheek this time."
Oh, with all that I've done wrong,
I must have done something right
To deserve her love every morning
And butterfly kisses at night.

Verse 3:
She'll change her name today.
She'll make a promise, and I'll give her away.
Standing in the bride room just staring at her,
She asks me what I'm thinking, and I say, "I'm not sure.
I just feel like I'm losing my baby girl."
Then she leaned over and gave me...

Chorus 3:
Butterfly kisses with her mama there,
Stickin' little white flowers all up in her hair.
"Walk me down the aisle, daddy, it's just about time."
"Does my wedding gown look pretty, daddy?
Daddy, don't cry."
Oh, with all that I've done wrong,
I must have done womething right
To deserve her love every morning
And butterfly kisses. *(Coda)*

BY HEART

Composed by
JIM BRICKMAN and
HOLLYE LEVEN
Arranged by DAN COATES

Hold me close,_____ ba - by, please._____
When you go,_____ I'll stop the clock.

Tell me an - - y - thing but that you're gon - na leave._____
I won't ev - er let this mo - ment stop._____

As I kiss_____ this fall - en tear,_____ I
Time is steal - in' you from me,_____ but it can

COUNT ON ME

Words and Music by
BABYFACE, WHITNEY HOUSTON
and **MICHAEL HOUSTON**
Arranged by DAN COATES

Count on Me - 3 - 1

Count on Me - 3 - 2

FOOLISH GAMES

Words and Music by
JEWEL KILCHER
Arranged by DAN COATES

44

Verse 2:
You're always the mysterious one
With dark eyes and careless hair,
You were fashionably sensitive
But too cool to care.
You stood in my doorway with nothing to say
Besides some comment on the weather.
(To Bridge:)

Verse 3:
You're always brilliant in the morning,
Smoking your cigarettes and talking over coffee.
Your philosophies on art, Baroque moved you.
You loved Mozart and you'd speak of your loved ones
As I clumsily strummed my guitar.

Verse 4:
You'd teach me of honest things,
Things that were daring, things that were clean.
Things that knew what an honest dollar did mean.
I hid my soiled hands behind my back.
Somehwere along the line,
I must have gone off track with you.

Bridge 2:
Excuse me, I think I've mistaken you
For somebody else, somebody who gave a damn,
Somebody more like myself.
(To Chorus:)

HOW DO I LIVE

Words and Music by
DIANE WARREN
Arranged by DAN COATES

Moderately slow

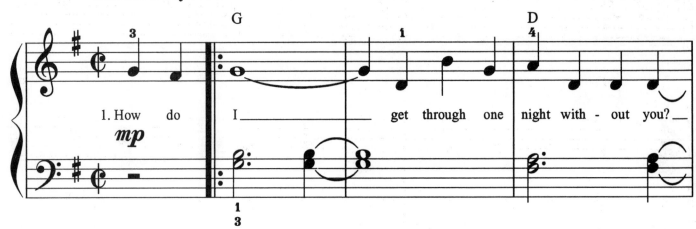

1. How do I _____ get through one night with - out you? _____

_____ If I had to live with - out you, _____ what kind of

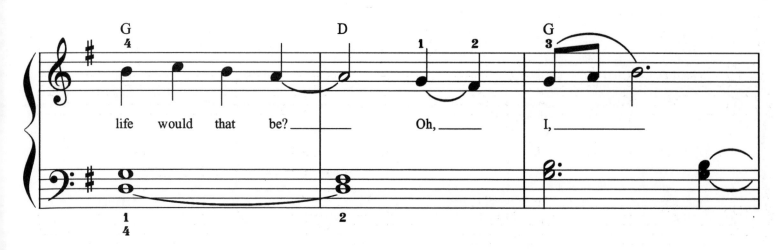

life would that be? _____ Oh, _____ I, _____

How Do I Live - 4 - 1

48

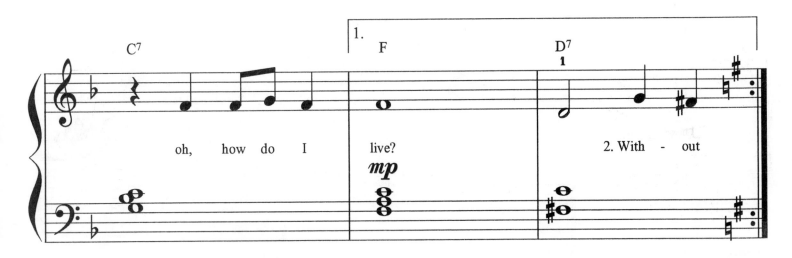

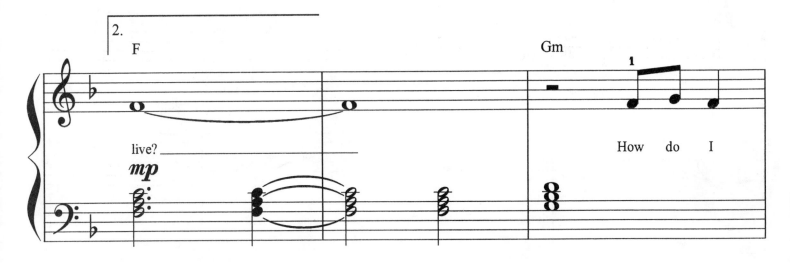

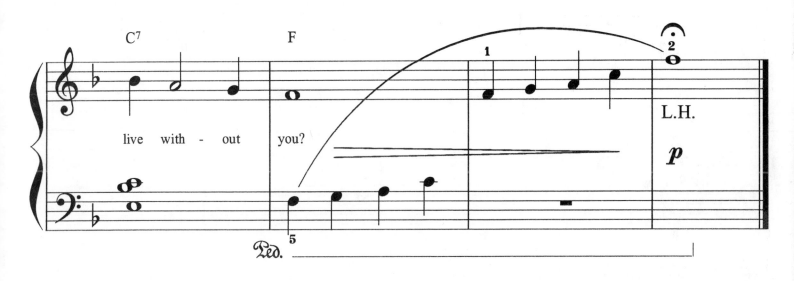

Verse 2:
Without you, there'd be no sun up in my sky,
There would be no love in my life,
There'd be no world left for me.
And I, baby, I don't know what I would do,
I'd be lost if I lost you.
If you ever leave,
Baby, you would take away everything
Real in my life.
And tell me now...
(To Chorus:)

I BELIEVE I CAN FLY

Words and Music by
R. KELLY
Arranged by DAN COATES

FROM THIS MOMENT ON

Words and Music by
SHANIA TWAIN and R.J. LANGE
Arranged by DAN COATES

Moderately slow

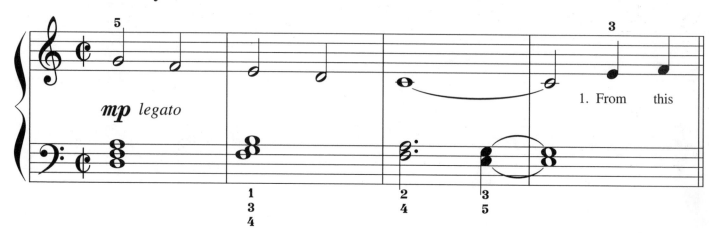

From This Moment On - 5 - 1

C
mo - ment, as long as I live, I will
F G7
love you, I pro - mise you this. there is
F C Dm
noth - ing I would - n't give, from this
G7 F
mo - ment. I will love you as long as I live,

Verse 3:
From this moment,
As long as I live,
I will love you,
I promise you this.
There is nothing
I wouldn't give,
From this moment on.

Chorus 2:
You're the reason I believe in love.
And you're the answer to my prayers
From up above.
All we need is just the two of us.
My dreams came true
Because of you.

From the Motion Picture "THE PREACHER'S WIFE"

I BELIEVE IN YOU AND ME

Words and Music by
SANDY LINZER and DAVID WOLFERT
Arranged by DAN COATES

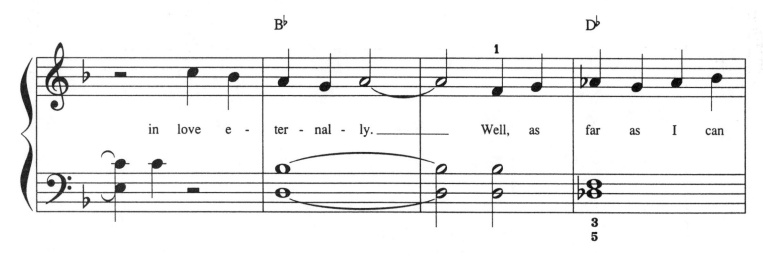

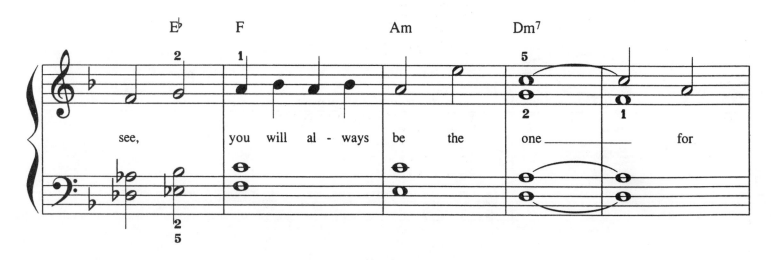

I Believe in You and Me - 5 - 1

I Believe in You and Me - 5 - 3

lost, _____ now I'm free, _____ 'cause

I be - lieve in you and me.

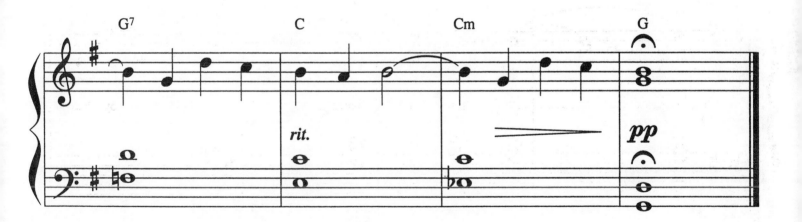

Verse 2:
I will never leave you side,
I will never hurt your pride.
When all the chips are down,
I will always be around
Just to be right where you are, my love.
Oh, I love you, boy.
I will never leave you out,
I will always let you in
To places no one has ever been.
Deep inside, can't you see?
I believe in you and me.

From Touchstone Pictures' ''ARMAGEDDON''

I DON'T WANT TO MISS A THING

Words and Music by
DIANE WARREN
Arranged by DAN COATES

I Don't Want to Miss a Thing - 4 - 1

I just wan-na hold you close, feel your heart so close to mine,

and just stay here in this mo-ment for all the rest of time.

Ba - by, ba - by.

D.S. 𝄋 al Coda

Coda

I Don't Want to Miss a Thing - 4 - 4

I LOVE YOU ALWAYS FOREVER

Words and Music by
DONNA LEWIS
Arranged by DAN COATES

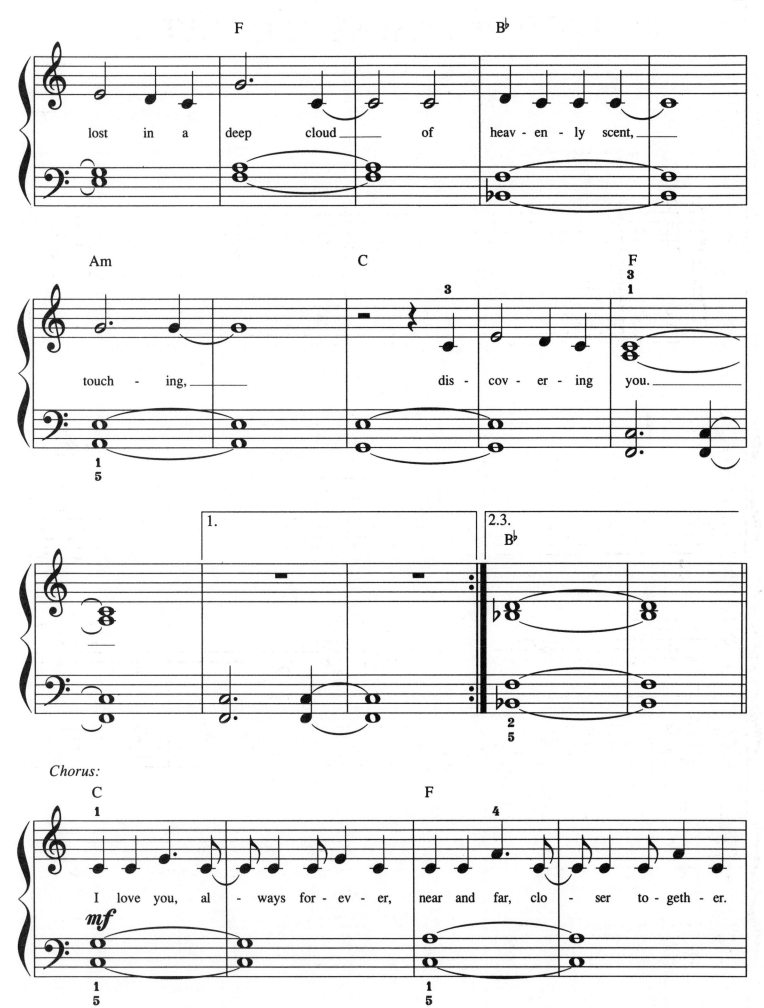

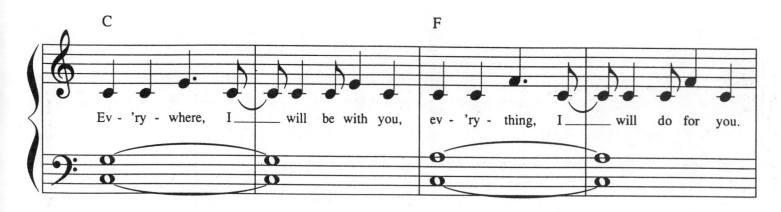

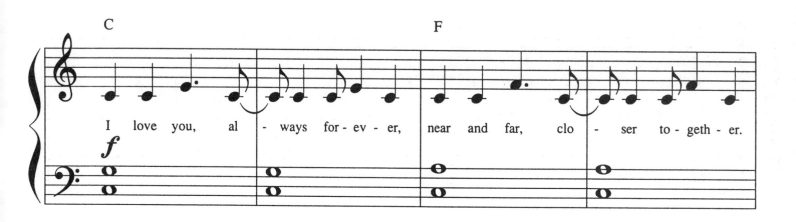

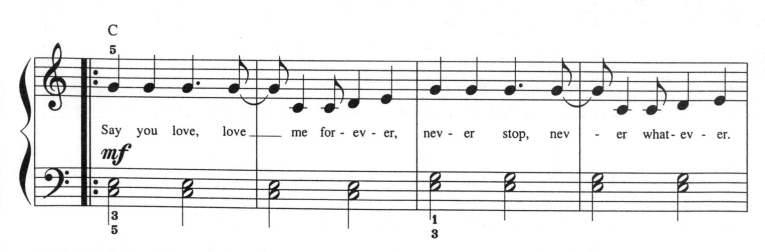

I Love You Always Forever - 4 - 3

Verse 2:
Thoses days of warm rain come rushing back to me,
Miles of windless, summer night air.
Secret moments shared in the heat of the afternoon,
Out of the stillness, soft spoken words. *(Chorus:)*

Verse 3:
You've got the most unbelievable blue eyes I've ever seen.
You've got me almost melting away as we lay there
Under blue sky with pure white stars,
Exotic sweetness, a magical time. *(Chorus:)*

From the Motion Picture "THE MIRROR HAS TWO FACES"

I FINALLY FOUND SOMEONE

Words and Music by
**BARBRA STREISAND, MARVIN HAMLISCH,
R.J. LANGE and BRYAN ADAMS**
Arranged by DAN COATES

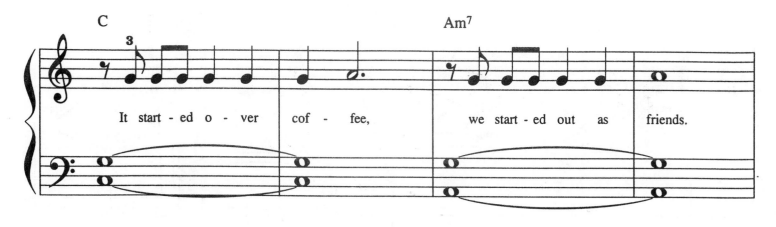

C   Am7

It start - ed o - ver cof - fee, we start - ed out as friends.

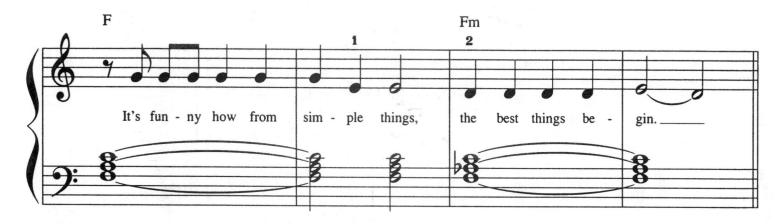

F   Fm

It's fun - ny how from sim - ple things, the best things be - gin. _____

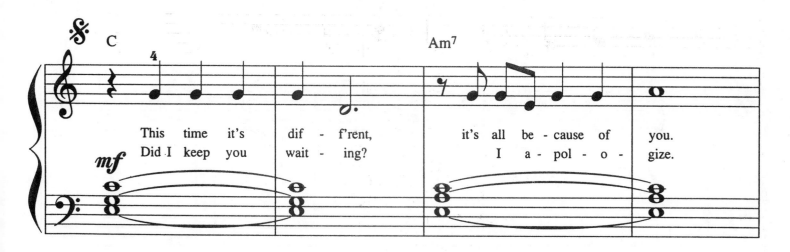

C   Am7

This time it's dif - f'rent, it's all be - cause of you.
Did I keep you wait - ing? I a - pol - o - gize.

mf

F   Fm

It's bet - ter than it's ev - er been 'cause we can talk it through. ____
I will wait for - ev - er just to know you were mine. _____

I Finally Found Someone - 5 - 2

I'LL BE THERE FOR YOU
Theme From "FRIENDS"

Words by
DAVID CRANE, MARTA KAUFFMAN, ALLEE WILLIS,
PHIL SOLEM and DANNY WILDE

Music by
MICHAEL SKLOFF
Arranged by DAN COATES

I'll Be There For You - 3 - 1

78

I'll Be There For You - 3 - 2

I SAY A LITTLE PRAYER

Words by
HAL DAVID

Music by
BURT BACHARACH
Arranged by DAN COATES

Brightly

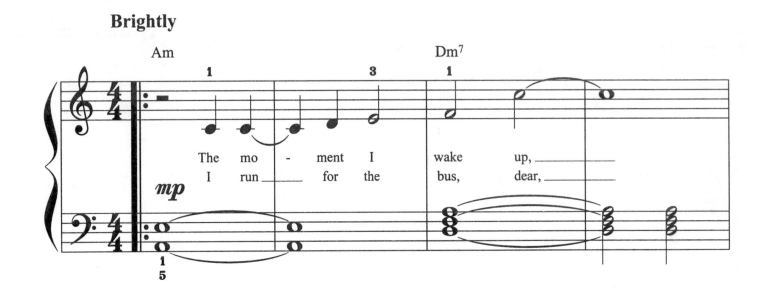

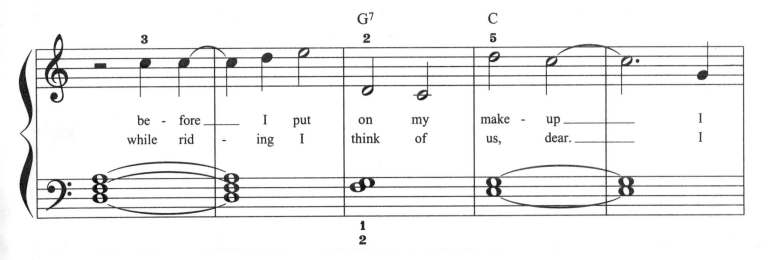

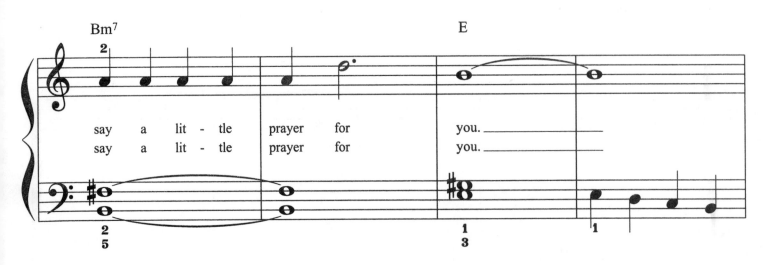

I Say a Little Prayer - 4 - 1

I WILL COME TO YOU

Words and Music by
ISAAC HANSON, TAYLOR HANSON, ZACHARY HANSON,
BARRY MANN and CYNTHIA WEIL
Arranged by DAN COATES

Moderately slow

When you have no light to guide you, and no one to walk be-
mp

side you, I will come to you, come ____ to you.

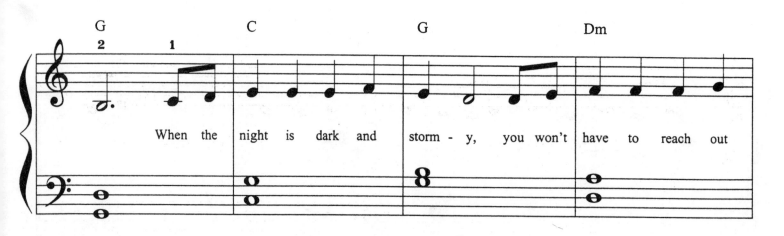

When the night is dark and storm-y, you won't have to reach out

I Will Come to You - 4 - 1

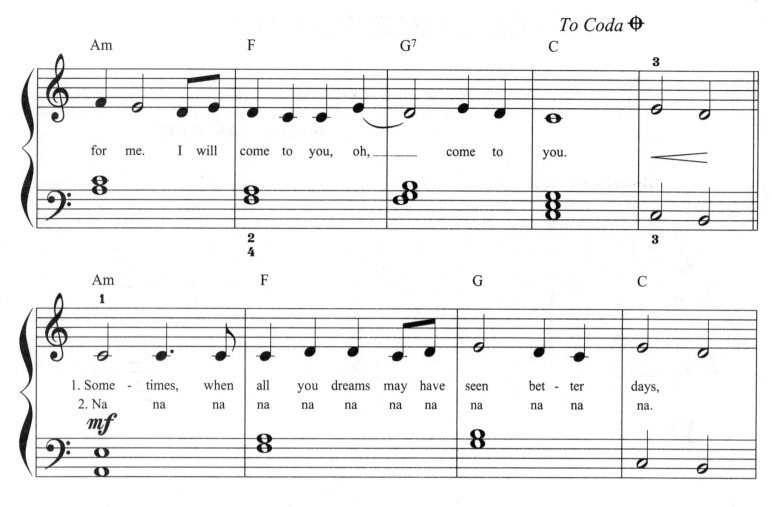

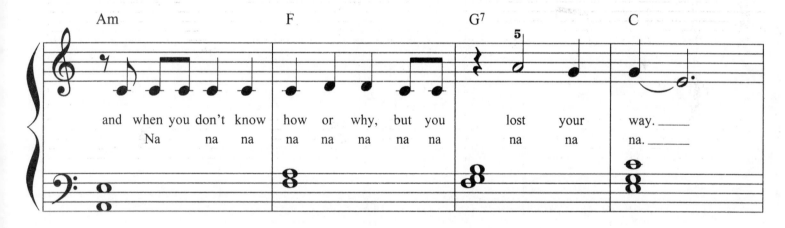

86

I Will Come to You - 4 - 3

I Will Come to You - 4 - 4

I'LL NEVER BREAK YOUR HEART

By
ALBERT MANNO and
EUGENE WILDE
Arranged by DAN COATES

Moderately slow

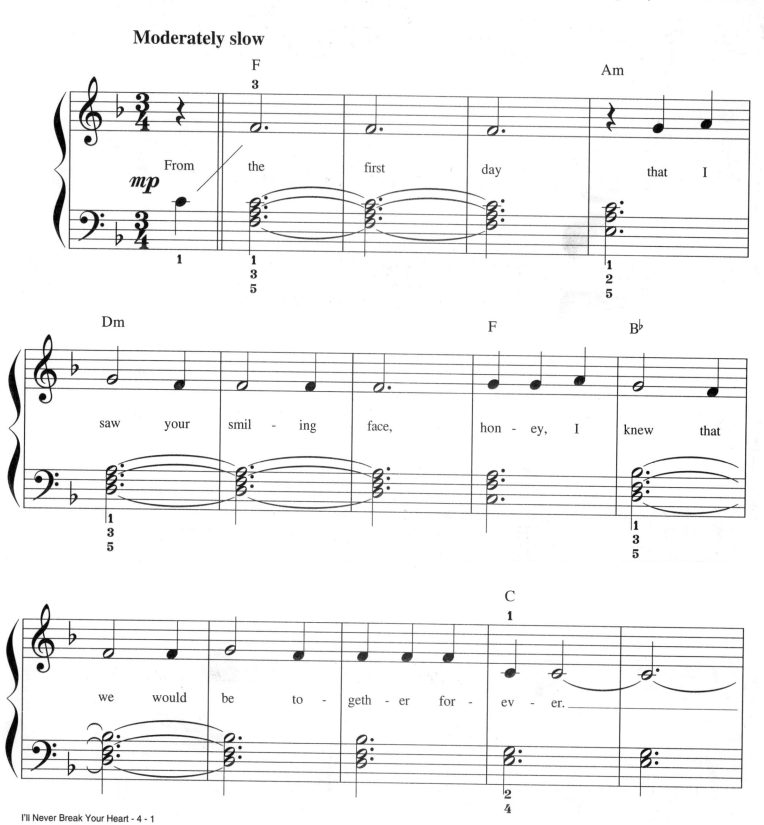

I'll Never Break Your Heart - 4 - 2

I'M YOUR ANGEL

Words and Music by
R. KELLY
Arranged by DAN COATES

94

I'm Your Angel - 5 - 3

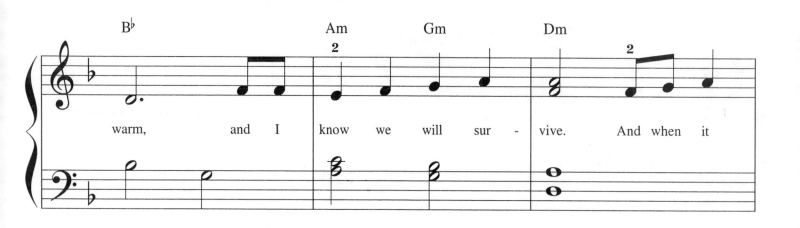

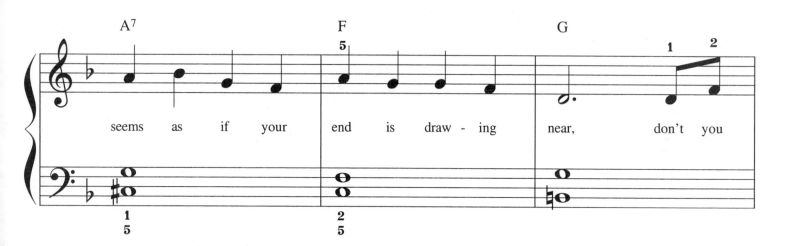

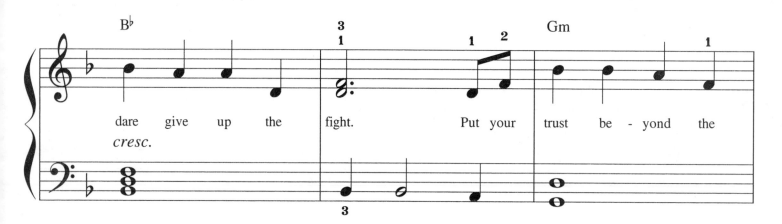

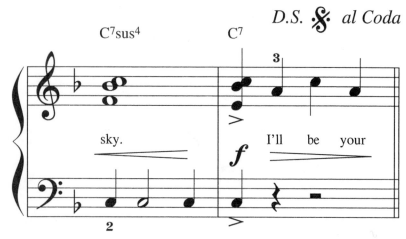

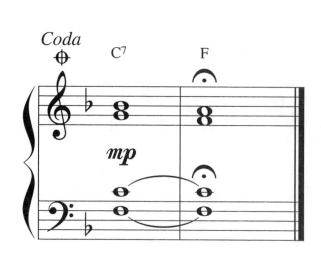

From the Twentieth Century-Fox Motion Picture "ANASTASIA"

JOURNEY TO THE PAST

Lyrics by
LYNN AHRENS

Music by
STEPHEN FLAHERTY
Arranged by DAN COATES

Not too fast

Heart don't fail me now.
Some - where down this road

Cour - age, don't de - sert me!
I know some - one's wait - ing.

Don't turn back now that we're here.
Years of dreams just can't be wrong.

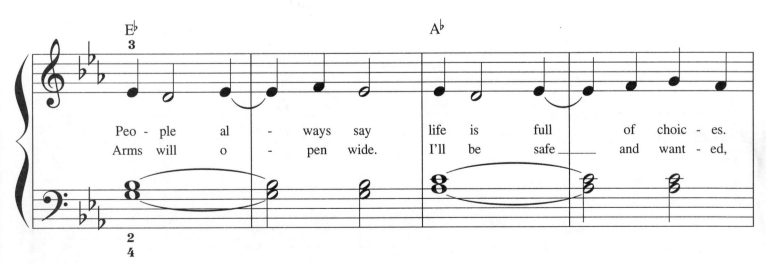

Peo - ple al - ways say life is full of choic - es.
Arms will o - pen wide. I'll be safe and want - ed,

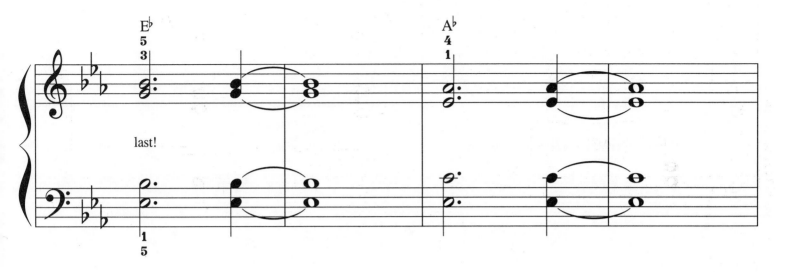

last!

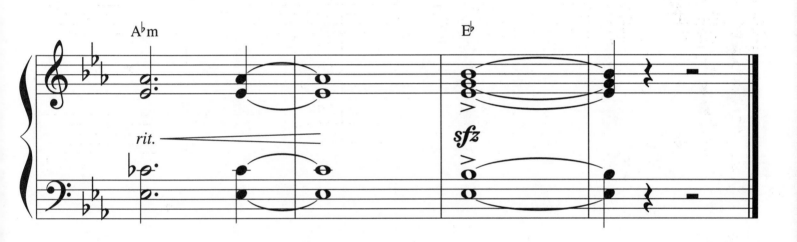

rit.

sfz

Verse 3:
One step at a time.
One hope, then another.
Who knows where this road may go.
Back to who I was.
On to find my future.
Things my heart still needs to know.
(To Coda:)

KAREN'S THEME

Composed by
RICHARD CARPENTER
Arranged by DAN COATES

Slowly, with expression

Karen's Theme - 3 - 1

D.C. al Coda

104

KISS THE RAIN

Words and Music by
ERIC BAZILIAN, DESMOND CHILD
and BILLIE MYERS
Arranged by DAN COATES

106

Kiss the Rain - 5 - 2

Kiss the Rain - 5 - 3

108

Kiss the Rain - 5 - 4

Verse 2:
Hello? Do you miss me?
I hear you say you do,
But not the way I'm missing you.
What's new? How's the weather?
Is it stormy where you are?
You sound so close,
But it feels like you're so far.
Oh, would it mean anything
If you knew what I'm left imagining
In my mind, in my mind.
Would you go, would go...
(To Chorus:)

LOOKING THROUGH YOUR EYES

Words and Music by
CAROLE BAYER SAGER
and DAVID FOSTER
Arranged by DAN COATES

Moderately slow

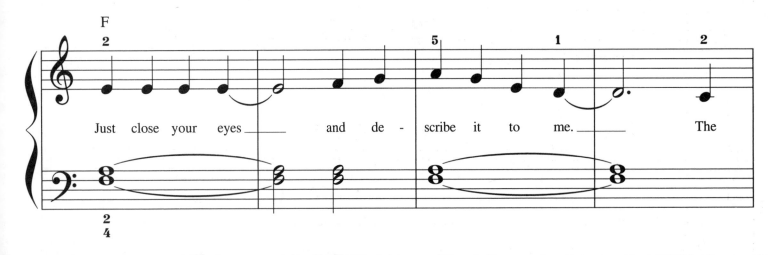

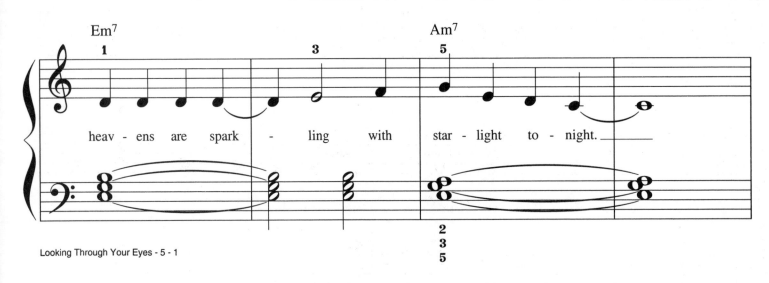

Looking Through Your Eyes - 5 - 1

114

Verse 2:
I see the heavens each time that you smile.
I hear your heartbeat just go on for miles,
And suddenly I know why life is worthwhile.
That's what I see through your eyes.
(To Chorus:)

Verse 3:
I look at myself and instead I see us.
Wherever I am now, it feels like enough.
And I see a girl who is learning to trust.
That's what I see through your eyes.
(To Chorus:)

MY ONE TRUE FRIEND
(From "ONE TRUE THING")

Words and Music by
CAROLE BAYER SAGER, CAROLE KING
and DAVID FOSTER
Arranged by DAN COATES

Slowly, with expression

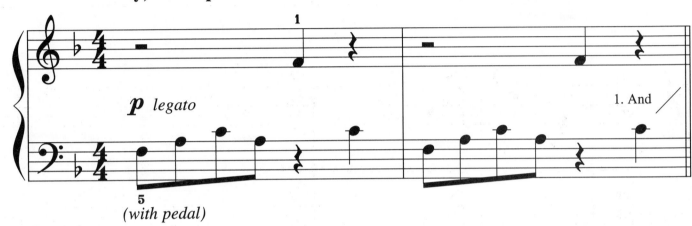

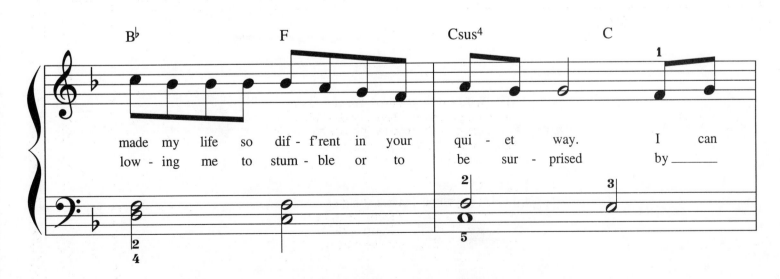

ONE OF US

Words and Music by
ERIC BAZILIAN
Arranged by DAN COATES

One of Us - 3 - 1

One of Us - 3 - 2

THE POWER OF GOODBYE

Words and Music by
MADONNA CICCONE
and RICK NOWELS
Arranged by DAN COATES

Mid-tempo ballad

The Power of Goodbye - 5 - 1

124

The Power of Goodbye - 5 - 2

126

The Power of Goodbye - 5 - 4

THE PRAYER

Words and Music by
CAROLE BAYER SAGER
and DAVID FOSTER
Arranged by DAN COATES

Slowly, with expression

QUIT PLAYING GAMES
(With My Heart)

Words and Music by
MAX MARTIN and HERBERT CRICHLOW
Arranged by DAN COATES

Bright rock tempo

132

Quit Playing Games - 4 - 3

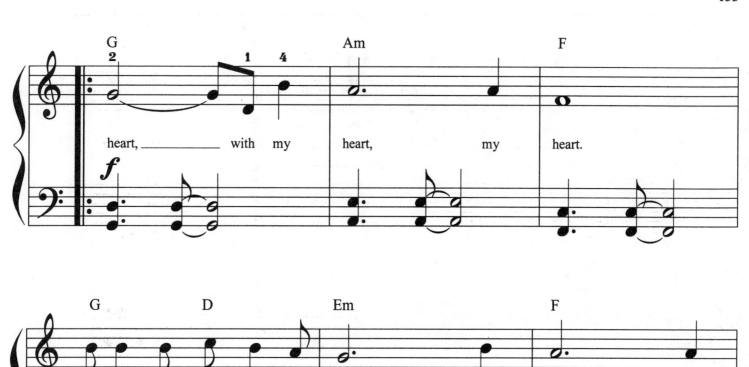

Verse 2:
I live my life the way,
To keep you comin' back to me.
Everything I do is for you,
So what is it that you can't see?
Sometimes I wish that I could turn back time,
Impossible as it may seem.
But I wish I could so bad, baby,
Quit playing games with my heart.

SOMETHING ABOUT THE WAY
YOU LOOK TONIGHT

Lyrics by
BERNIE TAUPIN

Music by
ELTON JOHN
Arranged by DAN COATES

136

Something About the Way You Look Tonight - 5 - 3

Something About the Way You Look Tonight - 5 - 4

STAR WARS
(Main Theme)

Music by
JOHN WILLIAMS
Arranged by DAN COATES

Majestically

Star Wars - 3 - 1

140

Star Wars - 3 - 3

TELL HIM

Words and Music by
LINDA THOMPSON, DAVID FOSTER
and WALTER AFANASIEFF
Arranged by DAN COATES

Slowly

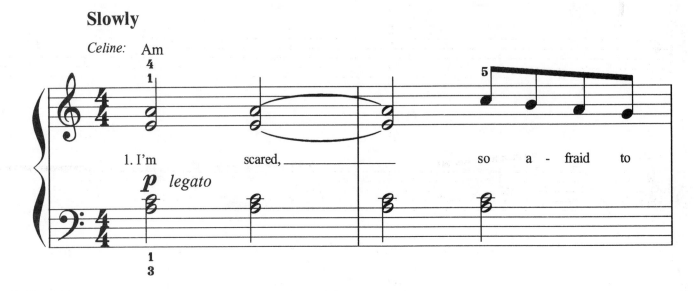

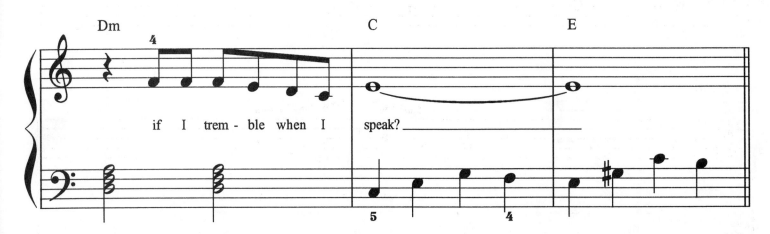

Tell Him - 5 - 1

144

Tell Him - 5 - 3

Verse 2:
(Barbra:)
Touch him with the gentleness you feel inside.
Your love can't be denied.
The truth will set you free.
You'll have what's meant to be.
All in time, you'll see.
(Celine:)
I love him,
Of that much I can be sure.
I don't think I could endure
If I let him walk away
When I have so much to say.
(To Chorus:)

UN-BREAK MY HEART

Words and Music by
DIANE WARREN
Arranged by DAN COATES

Moderately slow

THAT THING YOU DO!

Words and Music by
ADAM SCHLESINGER
Arranged by DAN COATES

Bright rock tempo

152

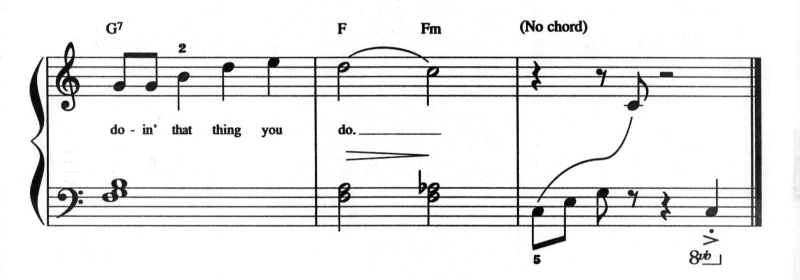

Verse 2:
I know all the games you play.
And I'm gonna find a way to let you know
That you'll be mine someday.
'Cause we could be happy, can't you see?
If you'd only let me be the one to hold you
And keep you here with me.
'Cause I try and try to forget you, girl,
But it's just too hard to do.
Every time you do that thing you do.

Verse 3:
(8 Bar Instrumental Solo...)
'Cause we could be happy, can't you see?
If you'd only let me be the one to hold you
And keep you here with me.
'Cause it hurts me so just to see you go
Around with someone new.
(To Coda:)

TIME TO SAY GOODBYE
(Con Te Partiró)

Lyrics by LUCIO QUARANTOTTO
English Lyrics by FRANK PETERSON

Music by FRANCESCO SARTORI
Arranged by DAN COATES

Time to Say Goodbye - 4 - 1

English literal translation:
Time to say goodbye.
Places that I've never seen
Or experienced with you,
Now I shall.
I'll sail with you upon ships across the seas,
Seas that exist no more.
It's time to say goodbye.

Time to Say Goodbye - 4 - 4

WALKIN' ON THE SUN

Words and Music by
STEVE HARWELL, GREGORY CAMP,
PAUL DeLISLE, and KEVIN COLEMAN
Arranged by DAN COATES

Moderately fast

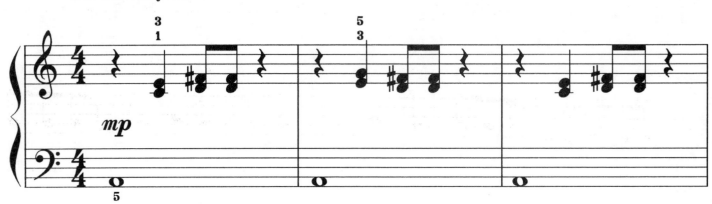

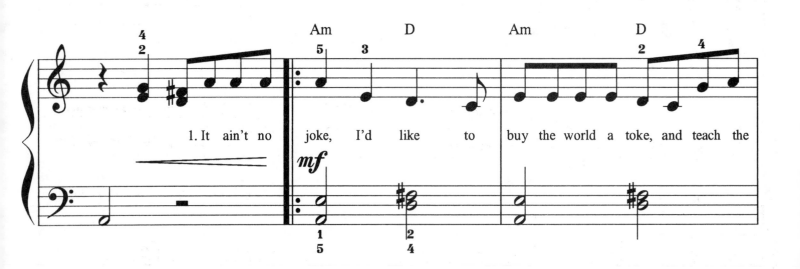

1. It ain't no joke, I'd like to buy the world a toke, and teach the

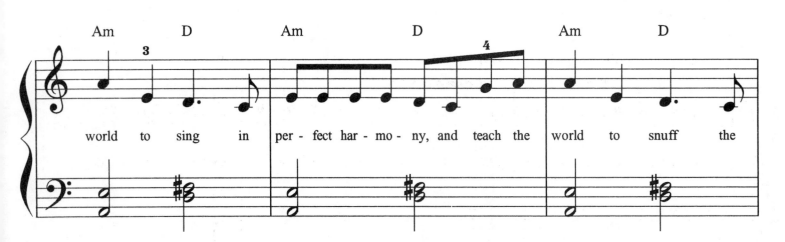

world to sing in per-fect har-mo-ny, and teach the world to snuff the

Walkin' on the Sun - 4 - 1

Verse 2:
Twenty-five years ago they spoke out
And they broke out of recession and oppression.
And together they toked and they folked out with guitars
Around a bonfire, just singin' and clappin', man, what the hell happened?
Yeah, some were spellbound, some were hell bound,
Some, they fell down and some got back up and fought back against the meltdown.
And their kids were hippie chicks, all hypocrites
Becasue their fashion is smashin' the true meaning of it.
(To Chorus:)

Verse 3:
It ain't no joke when a mama's handkerchief is soaked
With her tears because her baby's life has been revoked.
The bond is broke up, so choke up and focus on the close-up.
Mister Wizard can perform no god-like hocus pocus.
So don't sit back, kick back and watch the world get bushwacked.
News at ten, your neighborhood is under attack.
Put away the crack before the crack puts you away.
You need to be there when your baby's old enough to relate.
(To Chorus:)

WHAT IF

Words and Music by
DIANE WARREN
Arranged by DAN COATES

Moderately

Some - times _____ I don't un - der - stand,
Peo - ple, _____ they rush ev - 'ry - where.

feels like I'm liv - ing in a world gone mad. _____
No time to ev - er take the time to care. _____

Look a - round, _____ all a - round it's just the same.
We're the ones, _____ we're the los - ers in this game.

What If - 6 - 1

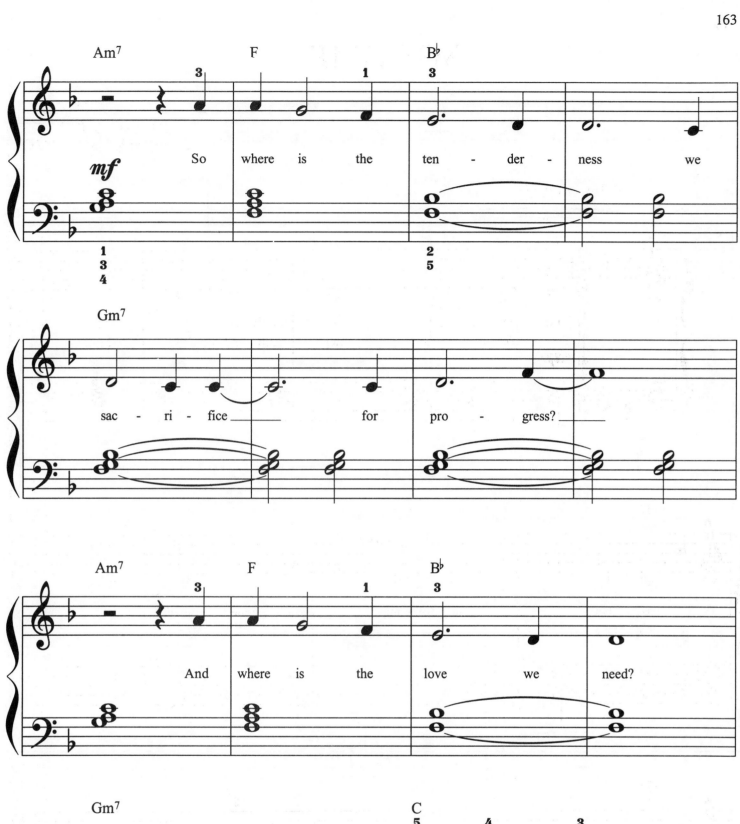

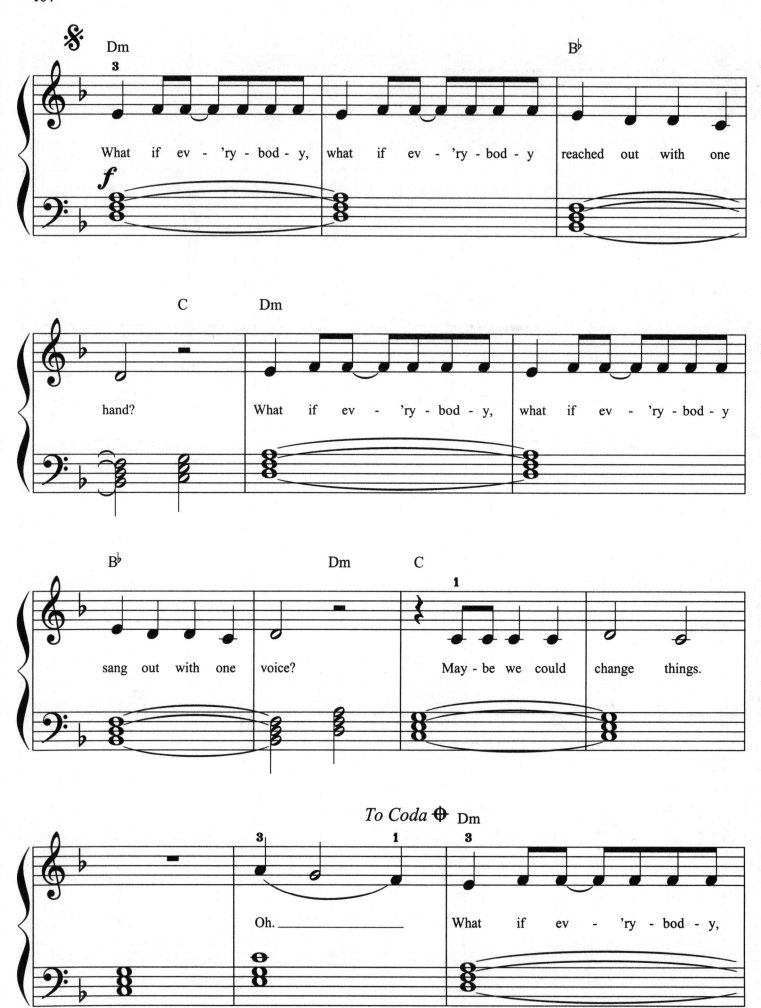

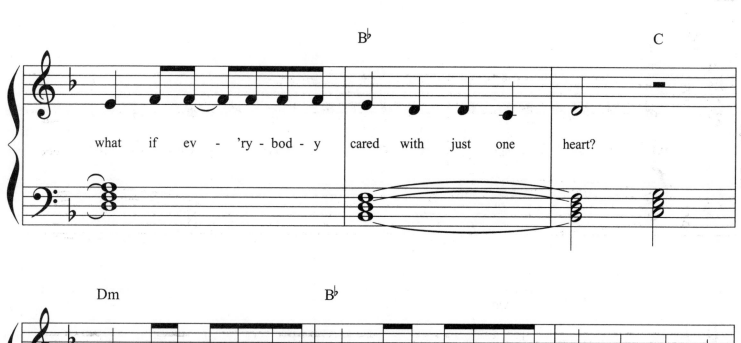

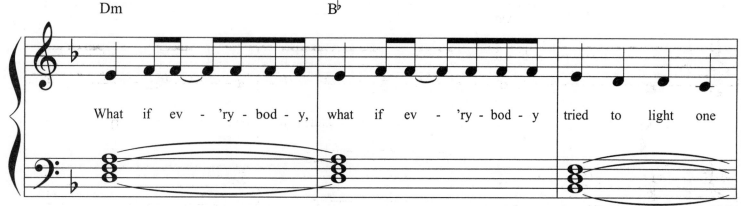

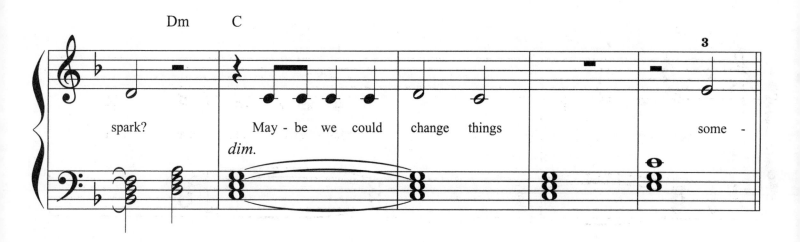

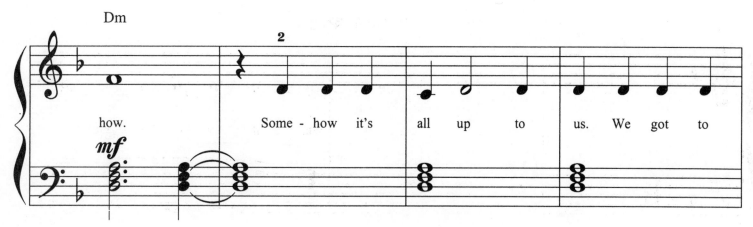

166

What If - 6 - 5

VALENTINE

Composed by
JIM BRICKMAN and JACK KUGELL
Arranged by DAN COATES

Valentine - 3 - 1

170

Verse 2:
All of my life,
I have been waiting for all you give to me.
You've opened my eyes
And shown me how to love unselfishly.
I've dreamed of this a thousand times before,
But in my dreams I couldn't love you more.
I will give you my heart until the end of time.
You're all I need, my love,
My Valentine.

YOU WERE MEANT FOR ME

Words and Music by
JEWEL KILCHER and STEVE POLTZ
Arranged by DAN COATES

Moderate swing feel

You Were Meant for Me - 5 - 1

172

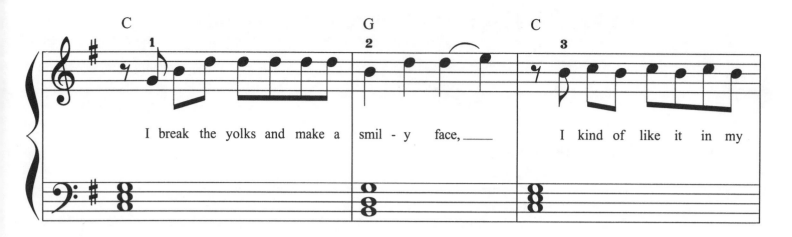

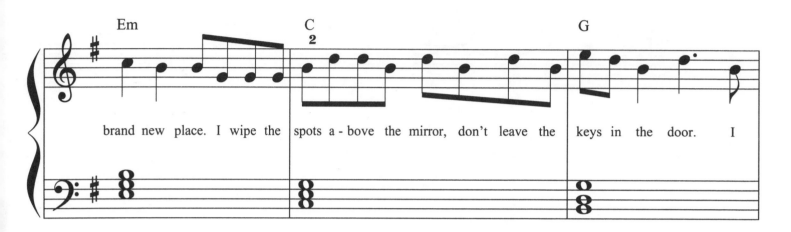

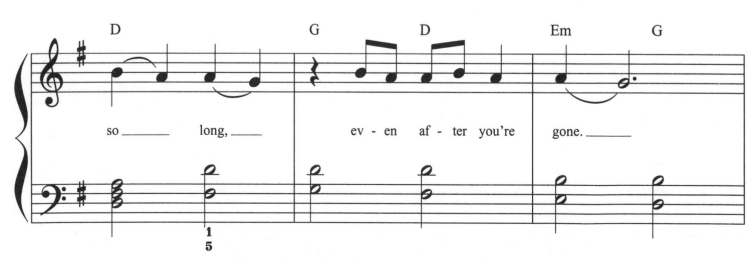

meant for me and I was meant for you.

Verse 2:
I called my mama, she was out for a walk.
Consoled a cup of coffee, but it didn't wanna talk.
So I picked up a paper, it was more bad news,
More hearts being broken or people being used.
Put on my coat in the pouring rain.
I saw a movie, it just wasn't the same,
'Cause it was happy and I was sad,
And it made me miss you, oh, so bad.
(To Chorus:)

Verse 3:
I brush my teeth and put the cap back on.
I know you hate it when I leave the light on.
I pick a book up and then I turn the sheets down,
And then I take a breath and a good look around.
Put on my pj's and hop into bed.
I'm half alive but I feel mostly dead.
I try and tell myself it'll be all right,
I just shouldn't think anymore tonight.
(To Chorus:)

DAN COATES

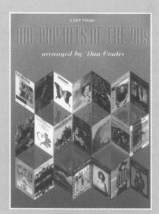

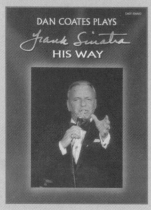
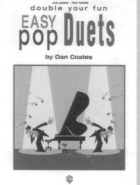
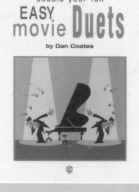